The Blue Swallows

H
N

The
Blue
Swallows

Poems by
Howard Nemerov

THE UNIVERSITY OF CHICAGO PRESS
CHICAGO & LONDON

One or more of these poems have appeared in the following publications, to whose editors grateful acknowledgment is made: the *American Scholar*, the *Atlantic Monthly*, *Approach*, the *Boston Review*, the *Carleton Miscellany*, *Folio* (Brandeis University), the *Harvard Advocate*, *Holiday*, the *Hollins Critic*, the *Island*, the *Kenyon Review*, the *Nation*, *Northwestern Tri-Quarterly*, the *Penny Paper*, *Polemic* (Western Reserve), the *Reporter*, *Shenandoah*, *Silo* (Bennington College), *Southern Poetry Review*, *Vassar Review*, and in student publications of the University of Vermont and Richmond University. The following poems first appeared in *The New Yorker:* 'The View,' 'The Companions,' 'At the Airport,' 'Presidential Address to a Party of Exiles,' 'The May Day Dancing,' and 'The Mud Turtle.' Several other of the poems have appeared in limited editions issued by the Tinker Press, Poems in Folio, the Perishable Press, and the Lowell-Adams House Printers.

Library of Congress Catalog Number: 67-25516
THE UNIVERSITY OF CHICAGO PRESS, CHICAGO 60637
The University of Chicago Press, Ltd., London W.C.1

To Margaret

To Margaret

Contents

III *Figures*

Part I

Legends

The First Day

Below the ten thousand billionth of a centimeter
Length ceases to exist. Beyond three billion light years
The nebulae would have to exceed the speed of light
In order to be, which is impossible: no universe.
The long and short of it seems to be that thought
Can make itself unthinkable, and that measurement
Of reach enough and scrupulosity will find its home
In the incommensurable. We shall not, nonetheless,
Admit to our discourse a Final Cause, but only
Groucho Marx, who said, "Closer? Any closer, lady,
And I'll be standing behind you." Now we're in the movies,
It may be said that within limits the Creation is
A going concern, imaginable because the film supplies
An image, a thin but absolute membrane whose surfaces
Divide the darkness from the light while at the same time
Uniting light and darkness, and whose linear motion,
Divided into frames, or moments, is at the same time
Continuous with itself and may be made to pace itself
Indistinguishably from the pace of time; being also
Able to be repeated, speeded up, slowed down, stopped,
And even run backwards, its model represents to us
Memory, concentration, causal sequence, analysis,
Time's irreversibility together with our doubt of this,
And a host of notions that from time long out of mind
Belong to the mind. That was the first day, and in that day
Of pure distinction, movies were without color, without sound.
Much later, words began to issue from the silence, and
The single light broke into spectral iridescence;
Meanwhile, in black and white and meddling into gray
Results, the Fall already is recorded on the film.
For "nothing in the universe can travel at the speed
Of light," they say, forgetful of the shadow's speed.

Creation of Anguish

Whatever sleeping in the world awakes,
We are the ones who to become ourselves
Awaken it, we are the ones who reach
Forever further, where the forest and the sky
And the incessantly restless sea invite
The voice that tells them fables of themselves
Till they shall make antiphonal response,
Confirming or else violently denying:
The hurricane's correction, or the fire
At night that scribbles out a city state.

Great pain was in the world before we came.
The shriek had learned to answer to the claw
Before we came; the gasp, the sigh, the groan,
Did not need our invention. But all these
Immediacies refused to signify
Till in the morning of the mental sun
One moment shuddered under stress and broke
Irreparably into before and after,
Inventing patience, panic, doubt, despair,
And with a single thrust producing thought
Beyond the possible, building the vaults
Of debt and the high citadels of guilt,
The segregating walls of obligation,
All that imposing masonry of time
Secretly rooted at the earth's cracked hearth,
In the Vishnu schist and the Bright Angel shale,
But up aspiring past the visible sky.

So was the raw material of pain
First metamorphosed, by the human touch,
Into significance, whence every man
And every woman, every child, becomes
Communicant: Shall I get better, or die?
Will they bring the electrodes soon again?
No, tell me what you really think of me.
Hence from nose-picking to the Crucifixion
One terrible continuum extends
Binding disaster to discovery.

And so the dog first entered in the door,
Whining and cringing, till we learned from him
Something of sympathy. Before we could,
We'd learned to wait as the condemned man waits
For the first light, his darkness, in the east,
And as the hunter waits before his trap,
The theorist before his question, or
The boy before his first time with a girl.
We learned, the soldier says, to sweat it out.

Landscape with Figures

What a dream of a landscape!
Cries Mrs Persepolis, and I
Agree, my gaze follows hers
Out to the giant recumbent
Hills in their sullen haze
Brooding some brutal thought
As it were about myself &
Mrs Persepolis, who are now
Alone in a closed garden
With various flowers and bees
And a feeble fountain that drips
On a stone in a heart-shaped
Pool with a single leopard-
Like toad immobilized all
Morning at his predatory
Meditation, making me think
Mrs Persepolis not too old
With her bright voice and
Wrinkling skin at the wrist
Patterned in sunburnt diamonds
But still a game old girl
(And I a game old guy) good
For a tumble in the August
Grass right at the center
Of the dream of a landscape

Till I see her glittering eye
Has taken this thought exactly
As the toad's tongue takes a fly
So that we laugh and the moment
Passes but Mrs Persepolis
As the bees go about their business

And we go in to have lunch
(How cold the house, the sudden
Shade! I shiver, and Mrs
Persepolis shivers too, till
Her bangles bangle) my dear
Mrs Persepolis, beautiful
Exile from childhood, girl
In your rough and wrinkled
Sack suit, couldn't you cry
Over that funny moment when
We almost fell together
Into the green sleep of the
Landscape, the hooded hills
That dream us up & down?

The Distances They Keep

They are with us always, but they have the wit
To stay away. We are walking through the woods,
A sudden bush explodes into sparrows, they
Show no desire to become our friends.
So also with the pheasant underfoot
In the stubble field; and lazy lapwings rise
To give their slow, unanimous consent
They want no part of us, who dare not say,
Considering the feathers in our caps,
They are mistaken in the distances they keep.

Still, the heart goes out to them. Goes out,
But maybe it's better this way. Let them stay
Pieces of world we're not responsible for,
Who can be killed by cleverness and hate,
But, being shy enough, may yet survive our love.

Learning by Doing

They're taking down a tree at the front door,
The power saw is snarling at some nerves,
Whining at others. Now and then it grunts,
And sawdust falls like snow or a drift of seeds.

Rotten, they tell us, at the fork, and one
Big wind would bring it down. So what they do
They do, as usual, to do us good.
Whatever cannot carry its own weight
Has got to go, and so on; you expect
To hear them talking next about survival
And the values of a free society.
For in the explanations people give
On these occasions there is generally some
Mean-spirited moral point, and everyone
Privately wonders if his neighbors plan
To saw him up before he falls on them.

Maybe a hundred years in sun and shower
Dismantled in a morning and let down
Out of itself a finger at a time
And then an arm, and so down to the trunk,
Until there's nothing left to hold on to
Or snub the splintery holding rope around,
And where those big green divagations were
So loftily with shadows interleaved
The absent-minded blue rains in on us.

Now that they've got it sectioned on the ground
It looks as though somebody made a plain
Error in diagnosis, for the wood
Looks sweet and sound throughout. You couldn't know,
Of course, until you took it down. That's what
Experts are for, and these experts stand round
The giant pieces of tree as though expecting
An instruction booklet from the factory
Before they try to put it back together.

Anyhow, there it isn't, on the ground.
Next come the tractor and the crowbar crew
To extirpate what's left and fill the grave.
Maybe tomorrow grass seed will be sown.
There's some mean-spirited moral point in that
As well: you learn to bury your mistakes,
Though for a while at dusk the darkening air
Will be with many shadows interleaved,
And pierced with a bewilderment of birds.

In the Commercial Gardens

Everything here has a price,
But one is allowed to come and look for nothing

Through the green warm wet alleys
Set forth with flowers, leaves, and ferns,

Experiencing free of charge
The delicately allusive misremembered fragrances

And reading their Latin names,
Their American prices; and wander away

Down the rich, dark avenues
Of earth, where flowers, trees, and ornamental shrubs

Are given a casual going-over
By golden-liveried privately owned bees.

At the exhibit's end there is
Nothing, not so much definition as a fence,

The planted rows get smaller,
Scruffier, there seem to be more flies than bees,

And we stand in wilderness
Again. It would be easy enough to go away

Stealing a bush; but no,
We have been privileged to look for nothing,

And it is right that we return
To exit where we entered, nothing in our hands.

The Cherry Tree

The cherry tree, symmetrically branching
Into its green confusions, now lights up
Its many suns, that slowly into summer
Intensify from white to pink, and to blood red.

The lives it lives are not only its own,
But the birds come also, and all day long
The leaves rattle, the branches shake and creak,
The whole tree seems to tremble where it stands.

The squirrels too come to its darkness, they flow
Heavy as waves along the bending boughs;
Inside the clattering shadow round the trunk
You hear a heterodyne hum and whine

As the economy of a minor universe
Distributes its goods (birds tearing at cherries
Are given a bonus of bugs), and everything
Keeps going until everything is gone,

And green and silent stands the tree again,
Shading the bloody stones, the rotting flesh,
In a cool circle of darkness from the sun:
Depending, at the end, from the one sun.

A Life

Innocence?
In a sense.
In no sense!

Was that *it*?
Was *that* it?
Was that it?

That was it.

Growing a Ghost

From the time he knew
he groomed his hair
in a gray pompadour
and made grim his smile
fitly to represent
all that would be meant
when he arrived by growing
to that great dignity
non-denominational
but solemn all the same
and showing forth a force—
   the stone jaw
   the sharp nose
   the closed lids

              dreaming
nightmares for all
who looked their last

looking his best
the ancestral look
in evening clothes
to go underground
and have at last
in his folded hands
the peace of the world

the red clay

Epitaph

Crazy, girls, crazy. Don is gone.
He was bucking for second circle
Along with Dido and Semiramis
And those kids reading of Lancelot
On a rainy afternoon. Think
Of Don sobbing on that dark wind.

The View

Under his view the wind
Blows shadows back and forth
Across the lawn beneath
The blowing leaves. And now
Into his silent room
Noon whistles, or a cry
Comes from the road where to
Is fro. Inquietude!
He walks from room to room,
From empty room to room
With the white curtains blowing.
He goes down to the kitchen
And takes from the cold tap
A glass of water pale
As glass. In the long hall
He stares into the mirror
And wills that it should break
Under his image, but
It does not break. Once more
He comes to stand before
The window and the screen,
Framing as in a graph
The view he has of flowers,
Of fields beyond the flowers,
The hanging hill, the blue
Distance that voids his vision
Though not as tears might do.

He has no tears, but knows
No one will come, there's no
Comfort, not the least
Saving discrepancy
In a view where every last thing
Is rimed with its own shadow
Exactly, and every fall
   Is once for all.

The Human Condition

In this motel where I was told to wait,
The television screen is stood before
The picture window. Nothing could be more
Use to a man than knowing where he's at,
And I don't know, but pace the day in doubt
Between my looking in and looking out.

Through snow, along the snowy road, cars pass
Going both ways, and pass behind the screen
Where heads of heroes sometimes can be seen
And sometimes cars, that speed across the glass.
Once I saw world and thought exactly meet,
But only in a picture by Magritte,

A picture of a picture, by Magritte,
Wherein a landscape on an easel stands
Before a window opening on a land-
scape, and the pair of them a perfect fit,
Silent and mad. You know right off, the room
Before that scene was always an empty room.

And that is now the room in which I stand
Waiting, or walk, and sometimes try to sleep.
The day falls into darkness while I keep
The TV going; headlights blaze behind
Its legendary traffic, love and hate,
In this motel where I was told to wait.

The Companions

There used to be gods in everything, and now they've gone.
A small one I remember, in a green-gray stone,
Would watch me go by with his still eyes of a toad,
And in the branch of an elm that hung across the road
Another was; he creaked at me on windless days.
Now that he's gone I think he might have wanted praise
For trying to speak my language and getting that far at least
Along on the imitation of a speaking beast.

Maybe he wanted help, maybe they all cried out
As they could, or stared helpless to enter into thought
With "read me," "answer me," or "teach me how to be
Whatever I am, and in return for teaching me
I'll tell you what I was in you, how greater far
Than I are seeking you in fountain, sun, and star."
That's but interpretation, the deep folly of man
To think that things can squeak at him more than things can.

And yet there came those voices up out of the ground
And got into my head, until articulate sound
Might speak them to themselves. We went a certain way
Together on that road, and then I turned away.

I must have done, I guess, to have grown so abstract
That all the lonely summer night's become but fact,
That when the cricket signals I no longer listen,
Nor read the glowworms' constellations when they glisten.

Sarajevo

In the summer, when the Archduke dies
Past the year's height, after the burning wheel
Steadies and plunges down the mountainside,
The days' succession fails from one to one
Still great as kings, whose shock troops in the field
Begin to burnish their green shoots to gold.

That undeclared war always takes the field
In the summer, when the Archduke dies,
And the blind spills buried beneath the wheel
Are risen, spears bespoken through earth's side
To sacrifice their fast and turning gold
In ransom for the blood of all in one.

Now that blood will be redeemed for gold
Eagle and crown aglitter in the wheel,
In the summer, when the Archduke dies,
Europe divides and fuses, side and side,
Ranging the human filings on the field
Of force, held by the magnet, not yet one.

Still empty of its food the battle field
Waits on the harvest and the great wain's wheel,
The vessels wait at hearth and harborside.
In the summer, when the Archduke dies,
Fate and the fortune of the game are one,
The green time turns to a heavy red, to gold.

And now responsible men on either side
Acknowledge their allegiance to the One
God of battles whose name is writ in gold,
The same whose coin, that cruelly blazing wheel,
In the summer, when the Archduke dies,
Buys earth as though it were a peasant's field.

The wildly streaming past now falls to one
Plunge on the oldest number of the wheel,
The zero twice redeemed in suicide,
Last blood sport of the green civilian field
Where the old world's sun went down in gold
In the summer when the Archduke died.

This, That & the Other

a dialogue in disregard

This: I stand and watch for minutes by the pond
        The snowflakes falling on the open water.
        Though I get cold, and though it tells me nothing,
        Or maybe just because it tells me nothing,
        I have to stand and watch the infinite white
        Particulate chaos of the falling snow
        Abolished in the black and waiting water.
        An instantaneous thing, time and again
        It happens, quicker than the eye can count:
        The snowflake drifting down erratically,
        Reflected for a second, suddenly
        Annihilated; no disturbance to
        The silent mirror spread beneath the sky.

That: I hasten to attend, I take it in.
        I think I see something of what you mean:
        It's just as Hermes Trismegistus said
        (Or as the scholars say that Hermes said),
        The things below are as the things above.
        A parable of universal love,
        To see the water taking in the snow
        Like that, a something neither quick nor slow,
        Eternal in an instant, as the All
        Unchanged receives the individual.

This: If that's the way you want it, courtesy
        Must say it's yours to make of what you will.
        But I was speaking only of the snow
        (They say that no two snowflakes are alike,
        How can they know?) touching the water's face
        So gently that to meet and melt are one.
        There's no more reason in it than in dreams.

That: Then I'll interpret you this dream of yours
          And make some sense of it; rather, of course,
          Some mind of it, for sense is what you make,
          And your provision is for me to take.
          First, I observe a pretty polarity
          Of black and white, and I ask, could this be
          A legend of the mingling of the races?
          The whites, with cold and isolated faces,
          Falling, a million Lucifers, out of
          Their self-made heaven into the primitive
          Beginnings that for centuries they hated,
          In fact into the undifferentiated?
          Political and metaphysical
          At once I read your little parable.

This: Water has many forms and still is water.
          The snow, the ice, the steam, the sailing cloud;
          Has many ways, between the raindrop and
          The great sea wave. One of the things it does
          Is mirror, and there's a model for all thought.

That: And more's to come, for mirroring reminds
          Me of Narcissus and his Echo, kinds
          One of the other, though unkind to him.
          Poor beauty pausing by the fountain's brim,
          Is he not imaged in the snowflake's last
          Moment of vanity, mirrored in the vast
          Abyss and yearning toward the steepdown gulf
          That seems to be, as it destroys, the self?

This: Echo, reflexion, radar of all sorts,
       The beauty of the mind is mediate,
       Its beauty and its sorrow. A poet said,
       Or had a political old fool say for him,
      "By indirections find directions out."
       A thought is thinking in my head: maybe
       The mind is not a spider, but a web.

That: The physicists are vexed between the wave
       And particle—would it not somehow save
       The appearances to think about the snow
       As particles becoming waves below,
       Exchanging not their natures but their shapes?
       And then, what's said of parity, perhaps
       That's pictured, and its overthrow as well,
       In this weakest of reactions: if, of all,
       One snowflake fell and somehow failed to drown
       But was deflected to the sky again . . .
       But there I'll stop, being compelled to see
       This isn't physics, but theology.

This: Sleeveless speculation, someone said,
       I disremember who, and never knew
       What it could mean. For even if a sleeve
       Could speculate, the arm of action still
       Would thrust a grasping hand out at the cuff,
       Bring morsels of this world up to the mouth
       To feed these dreams of immortality
       That end in death and defecation. See,
       The snow has stopped, the sun breaks out of cloud,
       A golden light is drifting through the glass.

That: A wind springs up that shatters images.

Both: The Other is deeply meddled in this world.
We see no more than that the fallen light
Is wrinkled in and with the wrinkling wave.

To a Scholar in the Stacks

When you began your story all its words
Had long been written down, its elements
Already so cohered in such exact
Equations that there should have seemed to be
No place to go, no entrance to the maze.
A heart less bold would have refused to start,
A mind less ignorant would have stayed home.

For Pasiphaë already had conceived
And borne her bully boy, and Daedalus
Responding had designed the darkness in
Its mystical divisions; Theseus,
Before you came, descended and returned,
By means of the thread, many and many a time.
What was there that had not been always done?

And still, when you began, only because
You did begin, the way opened before you.
The pictured walls made room, received your life;
Pasiphaë frowned, the Sea King greeted you,
And sighing Ariadne gave the thread
As always; in that celebrated scene
You were alone in being alone and new.

And now? You have gone down, you have gone in,
You have become incredibly rich and wise
From wandering underground. And yet you weary
And disbelieve, daring the Minotaur
Who answers in the echoes of your voice,
Holding the thread that has no other end,
Speaking her name whom you abandoned long ago.

Then out of this what revelation comes?
Sometimes in darkness and in deep despair
You will remember, Theseus, that you were
The Minotaur, the Labyrinth and the thread
Yourself; even you were that ingener
That fled the maze and flew—so long ago—
Over the sunlit sea to Sicily.

Lobsters

Here at the Super Duper, in a glass tank
Supplied by a rill of cold fresh water
Running down a glass washboard at one end
And siphoned off at the other, and so
Perpetually renewed, a herd of lobster
Is made available to the customer
Who may choose whichever one he wants
To carry home and drop into boiling water
And serve with a sauce of melted butter.

Meanwhile, the beauty of strangeness marks
These creatures, who move (when they do)
With a slow, vague wavering of claws,
The somnambulist's effortless clambering
As he crawls over the shell of a dream
Resembling himself. Their velvet colors,
Mud red, bruise purple, cadaver green
Speckled with black, their camouflage at home,
Make them conspicuous here in the strong
Day-imitating light, the incommensurable
Philosophers and at the same time victims
Herded together in the marketplace, asleep
Except for certain tentative gestures
Of their antennae, or their imperial claws
Pegged shut with a whittled stick at the wrist.

We inlanders, buying our needful food,
Pause over these slow, gigantic spiders
That spin not. We pause and are bemused,
And sometimes it happens that a mind sinks down
To the blind abyss in a swirl of sand, goes cold
And archaic in a carapace of horn,
Thinking: There's something underneath the world. . . .

The flame beneath the pot that boils the water.

An Old Colonial Imperialist

To grip through the ground with your feet;
To feel your toes curled around rocks,
Sucking up water; to stand up straight
And tall for a certain time, and after
Go off in any direction, so long as it's up;
That's what I call living: standing there.

Tons of water creeping up my stomach,
Immense strain in my many shoulders
Holding their limbs in proclamation;
When a starling lands in my hair
I know it; when the hairy woodpecker
Hits me for lice, I know where the lice are.
My patches of lichen itch for centuries,
I do not stoop to scratch; you pay
For dignity in this world.
                                    Grown old,
I suffer the surgeon's pruning bill,
Cement in my cavities, healing tar
Over my incidental stumps. I go on,
Bending a little in the bigger winds,
Waving light airs away, and every fall
I drop the year's familiarity
Of used leaves with a certain contempt.

Beyond the Pleasure Principle

It comes up out of the darkness, and it returns
Into a further darkness. After the monster,
There is the monster's mother to be dealt with,
Dimly perceived at first, or only speculated on
Between the shadows and reflexions of the tidal cave,
Among the bones and armored emptiness
Of the princes of a former time, who failed.

Our human thought arose at first in myth,
And going far enough became a myth once more;
Its pretty productions in between, those splendid
Tarnhelms and winged sandals, mirroring shields
And swords unbreakable, of guaranteed
Fatality, those endlessly winding labyrinths
In which all minotaurs might find themselves at home,
Deceived us with false views of the end, leaving
Invisible the obstinate residuum, so cloudy, cold,
Archaic, that waits beyond both purpose and fulfilment.

There, toward the end, when the left-handed wish
Is satisfied as it is given up, when the hero
Endures his cancer and more obstinately than ever
Grins at the consolations of religion as at a child's
Frightened pretensions, and when his great courage
Becomes a wish to die, there appears, so obscurely,
Pathetically, out of the wounded torment and the play,
A something primitive and appealing, and still dangerous,
That crawls on bleeding hands and knees over the floor
Toward him, and whispers as if to confess: *again, again.*

Departure of the Ships

The voyages always beginning, always ending,
Dreams of the past enacted in the future,
Autonomous, and dreamed by all and none:
Wars, oracles, sacrifices, necessary dominations
Of the driven by the driven; priestly lustrations
Of murdering hands now still in the dust as dust;
And history, the dream within a dream,
Endless, remorselessly detailed anamnesis
To justify the sufferings and the crimes
Of the unborn; the chanting, muttering, whispering
Digestion of the random in necessity,
The repetition that convicts and kills.

Wealth also, with its generations:
The circulation of the currency
Through ruble and crown, dollar and franc, blood
Of the public confidence, unlimited legend
Phantasied against original obligation
Of time unredeemable and time that grows
Impudent in the earthy vault, compounding interest
In the tidal periods of calendar and clock,
The silver of the moon and the sun's gold.

See now, the ships depart through the dark harbor
And past the breakwater rocks where the first
White-riding wave hits at the hull and washes on.
Rhythm of voyages, going out and coming back,
Beat of the sea, procession of times and seasons,
Command of variables, calculus of fluxions
Cuius Nomen est Oriens, keeping time
Where endless hours summon and dismiss,
The hours of adoration and revenge,

Of triumph, lamentation and despair,
Devoted hours of the iron and brazen bells
That swing in the steeple over the old Exchange,
Counting and keeping all that cannot be kept.

O star of the sea, naked and dangerous candor,
Blaze of the compass rose, our ships depart!
Iron hands of the clock meet and divide,
The white face on the tower looks to sea,
Where unaccountable sands cloudily sift
Through the salt black bitter glass that gives
Tidal ideas about time, and no tidings.

Part II

The Great Society

The Night before Christmas

I am buying presents for everyone.
It is very late, but better late,
They say, than never. I want
Everyone to be happy, but admit
I frequently do not do enough
To implement this wish. Now
It is late, December Twenty-Fourth
Darkens, and I, with others
Scourged by the same conviction
Of an absolute delinquency,
Am walking the cold avenue
Between the lines of brilliant windows
Filled with impersonal satisfactions.
I clutch my money, I shudder with cold,
I go on attempting to buy
The happiness of others.

(An ox at a crèche looks out,
And I look in. A small doll
In the cradle has closed eyes.
You will be crucified, Baby,
I croon, before going on,
And we will buy you, Baby,
Cathedrals for Christmas.)

Lovers, relations, friends,
And business acquaintances,
I swear to express my love
Somehow. Say what you want,
Say what would make you happy,
Before I spill my money in
The dark river as it ebbs

To sea, that its hurrying current
May devalue these my dollars
In depths beyond redemption,
And in the dragon's treasury
The price of prices be forgot,
And the potlatch of time.

Sunday

He rested on the seventh day, and so
The chauffeur had the morning off, the maid
Slept late, and cook went out to morning mass.
So by and large there was nothing to do
Among the ashtrays in the living room
But breathe the greyish air left over from
Last night, and go down on your knees to read
The horrible funnies flattened on the floor.

It's still a day to conjure with, if not
Against, the blessed seventh, when we get
A chance to feel whatever He must feel,
Looking us over, seeing that we are good.
The odds are six to one He's gone away;
It's why there's so much praying on this day.

Enthusiasm for Hats

Under their great hats the women walk
To Sunday service, all along the street
Among the secretive suburban houses
An amazement of hats, towering, askew,
Supported upon frames or cantilevered,
Held on by spikes or flying buttresses,
Hats bundled, hats bolstered, tea cozy hats
And hats huge that could cozy chamber pots,
Parades under the porches of the churches.

Hats must be pleasing in the sight of God.
As though they could have had no human maker
They rise in splendor, sway in independence,
Bobble and nod in glory above the heads
As manifestations from the mind itself,
Expressing the erection of pure thought
In velvet, pelt, and feather. O high hats!
As secret of significance as those
Dormers there at the peaks of private houses
Along these quiet streets, where people keep
Hidden in filth a broken relative.

A Way of Life

It's been going on a long time.
For instance, these two guys, not saying much, who slog
Through sun and sand, fleeing the scene of their crime,
Till one turns, without a word, and smacks
His buddy flat with the flat of an axe,
Which cuts down on the dialogue
Some, but is viewed rather as normal than sad
By me, as I wait for the next ad.

It seems to me it's been quite a while
Since the last vision of blonde loveliness
Vanished, her shampoo and shower and general style
Replaced by this lean young lunk-
head parading along with a gun in his back to confess
How yestereve, being drunk
And in a state of existential despair,
He beat up his grandma and pawned her invalid chair.

But here at last is a pale beauty
Smoking a filter beside a mountain stream,
Brief interlude, before the conflict of love and duty
Gets moving again, as sheriff and posse expound,
Between jail and saloon, the American Dream
Where Justice, after considerable horsing around,
Turns out to be Mercy; when the villain is knocked off,
A kindly uncle offers syrup for my cough.

And now these clean-cut athletic types
In global hats are having a nervous debate
As they stand between their individual rocket ships
Which have landed, appropriately, on some rocks
Somewhere in Space, in an atmosphere of hate

Where one tells the other to pull up his socks
And get going, he doesn't say where; they fade,
And an angel food cake flutters in the void.

I used to leave now and again;
No more. A lot of violence in American life
These days, mobsters and cops all over the scene.
But there's a lot of love, too, mixed with the strife,
And kitchen-kindness, like a bedtime story
With rich food and a more kissable depilatory.
Still, I keep my weapons handy, sitting here
Smoking and shaving and drinking the dry beer.

Money

an introductory lecture

This morning we shall spend a few minutes
Upon the study of symbolism, which is basic
To the nature of money. I show you this nickel.
Icons and cryptograms are written all over
The nickel: one side shows a hunchbacked bison
Bending his head and curling his tail to accommodate
The circular nature of money. Over him arches
UNITED STATES OF AMERICA, and, squinched in
Between that and his rump, E PLURIBUS UNUM,
A Roman reminiscence that appears to mean
An indeterminately large number of things
All of which are the same. Under the bison
A straight line giving him a ground to stand on
Reads FIVE CENTS. And on the other side of our nickel
There is the profile of a man with long hair
And a couple of feathers in the hair; we know
Somehow that he is an American Indian, and
He wears the number nineteen-thirty-six.
Right in front of his eyes the word LIBERTY, bent
To conform with the curve of the rim, appears
To be falling out of the sky Y first; the Indian
Keeps his eyes downcast and does not notice this;
To notice it, indeed, would be shortsighted of him.
So much for the iconography of one of our nickels,
Which is now becoming a rarity and something of
A collectors' item: for as a matter of fact
There is almost nothing you can buy with a nickel,
The representative American Indian was destroyed
A hundred years or so ago, and his descendants'
Relations with liberty are maintained with reservations,
Or primitive concentration camps; while the bison,

Except for a few examples kept in cages,
Is now extinct. Something like that, I think,
Is what Keats must have meant in his celebrated
Ode on a Grecian Urn.
                    Notice, in conclusion,
A number of circumstances sometimes overlooked
Even by experts: (*a*) Indian and bison,
Confined to obverse and reverse of the coin,
Can never see each other; (*b*) they are looking
In opposite directions, the bison past
The Indian's feathers, the Indian past
The bison's tail; (*c*) they are upside down
To one another; (*d*) the bison has a human face
Somewhat resembling that of Jupiter Ammon.
I hope that our studies today will have shown you
Something of the import of symbolism
With respect to the understanding of what is symbolized.

Make Love Not War

Lovers everywhere are bringing babies into the world.
Lovers with stars in their eyes are turning the stars
Into babies, lovers reading the instructions in comic books
Are turning out babies according to the instructions; this
Progression is said by demographers to be geometric and
Accelerating the rate of its acceleration. Lovers abed
Read up the demographers' reports, and accordingly produce
Babies with contact lenses and babies diapered in the flags
Of new and underdeveloped nations. Some experts contend
That bayonets are being put into the hands of babies
Not old enough to understand their use. And in the U.S.,
Treasury officials have expressed their grave concern about
The unauthorized entry of stateless babies without
Passports and knowing no English: these "wetbacks,"
As they are called from the circumstance of their swimming
Into this country, are to be reported to the proper
Authority wherever they occur and put through channels
For deportation to Abysmo the equatorial paradise
Believed to be their country of origin—"where,"
According to one of our usually unformed sorcerers,
"The bounteous foison of untilled Nature alone
Will rain upon the heads of these homeless, unhappy
And helpless beings apples, melons, honey, nuts, and gum
Sufficient to preserve them in their prelapsarian state
Under the benign stare of Our Lord Et Cetera forevermore."

Meanwhile I forgot to tell you, back at the ranch,
The lovers are growing older, becoming more responsible.
Beginning with the mortal courtship of the Emerald Goddess
By Doctor Wasp—both of them twelve feet high
And insatiable; he wins her love by scientific means
And she has him immolated in a specially designed mole—

45

They have now settled down in an L-shaped ranch-type home
Where they are running a baby ranch and bringing up
Powerful babies able to defend their Way of Life
To the death if necessary. Of such breeding pairs
The average he owns seven and a half pair of pants,
While she generally has three girdles and a stove.
They keep a small pump-action repeater in the closet,
And it will not go off in the last act of this epic.

To sum up, it was for all the world as if one had said
Increase! Be fruitful! Multiply! Divide!
Be as the sands of the sea, the stars in the firmament,
The moral law within, the number of molecules
In the unabridged dictionary. BVD. Amen. Ahem.

AUM.

(Or, roughly, the peace that passeth understanding.)

A Negro Cemetery Next to a White One

I wouldn't much object, if I were black,
To being turned away at the iron gate
By the dark blonde angel holding up a plaque
That said White Only; who would mind the wait

For those facilities? And still it's odd,
Though a natural god-given civil right,
For men to throw it in the face of God
Some ghosts are black and some darknesses white.

But since they failed to integrate the earth,
It's white of them to give what tantamounts
To it, making us all, for what that's worth,
Separate but equal where it counts.

At the Airport

Through the gate, where nowhere and night begin,
A hundred suddenly appear and lose
Themselves in the hot and crowded waiting room.
A hundred other herd up toward the gate,
Patiently waiting that the way be opened
To nowhere and night, while a voice recites
The intermittent litany of numbers
And the holy names of distant destinations.

None going out can be certain of getting there.
None getting there can be certain of being loved
Enough. But they are sealed in the silver tube
And lifted up to be fed and cosseted,
While their upholstered cell of warmth and light
Shatters the darkness, neither here nor there.

Presidential Address to a Party of Exiles

There are too many of you.
Heaven is closed. The Age
Of Reason is full up, too.
And we have no more jobs
For Romantic Poets. Go.

I shall think of you often
In your sterilized cocoons
Stilting about in the steel wool
Or whatever, spidering
Fastidiously over the gray dust
With your grieving fingers
That want to come home. But
There are too many of you.

You might have stayed with us
In the lattice of stonework,
In the crystalline fracture
Of cemeteries, and been among
Our memories, in the chalk
Dust of a blackboard's thought
A cloudy erasure, but
So many of you . . . ? Pilots,
Man your solipsisms,
Mahomet in his coffin not
More free. Go, voyagers,
I want you to know my thought
   Goes always with you.

To the Governor & Legislature of Massachusetts

When I took a job teaching in Massachusetts
I didn't know and no one told me that I'd have to sign
An oath of loyalty to the Commonwealth of Massachusetts.
Now that I'm hooked, though, with a house
And a mortgage on the house, the road ahead
Is clear: I sign. But I want you gentlemen to know
That till today it never once occurred to me
To overthrow the Commonwealth of Massachusetts
By violence or subversion, or by preaching either.
But now I'm not so sure. It makes a fellow think,
Can such things be? Can such things be in the very crib
Of our liberties, and East of the Hudson, at that?

So if the day come that I should shove the Berkshire Hills
Over the border and annex them to Vermont,
Or snap Cape Cod off at the elbow and scatter
Hyannis to Provincetown beyond the twelve-mile limit,
Proclaiming apocalypsopetls to my pupils
And with state troopers dripping from my fingertips
Squeaking "You promised, you broke your promise!"
You gentlemen just sit there with my signature
And keep on lawyer-talking like nothing had happened,
Lest I root out that wagon tongue on Bunker Hill
And fungo your Golden Dome right into Fenway Park
Like any red-celled American boy ought to done
Long ago in the first place, just to keep in practice.

A Full Professor

Surely there was, at first, some love of letters
To get him started on the routine climb
That brought him to this eminence in time?
But now he has become one of his betters.

He has survived, and even fattened on,
The dissertation and the discipline.
The eyes are spectacled, the hair is thin,
He is a dangerous committeeman.

An organism highly specialized,
He diets on, for daily bill of fare,
The blood of Keats, the mind of poor John Clare;
Within his range, he cannot be surprised.

Publish or perish! What a frightful chance!
It troubled him through all his early days.
But now he has the system beat both ways;
He publishes and perishes at once.

Grace To Be Said before Committee Meetings

The problem was to get first things
To come first, and when you had them first
To build, course after course,
In an orderly manner, the problem was,
Your tower. It wouldn't be easy,
Nobody ever said it would be easy,
But your reward would be, with first
Things first, order, the tower,
Majesty. How this would come about
Nobody ever said, and that was
The problem that so exercised
The best minds of that generation.

The last thing you get to know,
Pascal had said, is what comes first.

Of course, much had been done
Already, nobody ever said
It hadn't, but the problem was
Whether to tear it up, or build
On those shifty foundations.
So the best minds exercised
Mightily, and they decided
The past indeed had been full
Of error, nobody ever said
It wasn't, but as for them
Themselves, the answer was,
If they had been there back then,
When those things happened, that is,
They would not have happened because

They would not have let them happen,
Because they weren't the sort of guys
Who would have poisoned Socrates
Or crucified their Savior, and
By God nobody ever said they were.

A Relation of Art and Life

Into the sacred precincts come the savage sages,
The shamans meager of body, furious of mind
From lonesome meditations near to madness,
The wizards, wardens of the kindless wonders,
And prophets, who seek to bring catastrophe
Under a copyright, and doom to its publication.
With eyeballs able to swivel in their sockets,
These are the universal joints between the All and Nothing;
Driven by dreams to the interpreters of dreams,
They are without sin, and casting their first stones.

Out of the desert they come, and from the mountains,
From contemplation of those still sterilities
Or the repetition of the ocean tides deriving
Each one his remedy for men, his unpriced pearl
To sell to the priesthood to be a secret saying
To say over sacrifices, to be cast in contempt
Before popular swine. The secret sayings are such
As destroy societies; to have one is to hold
A hot coal in the mouth, and what mouth would stay closed?
The sages have arrived; they are breathing fire.

First, Sexual License, all sweat and dishevel
And a scrotum stuffed like the sack of Santa Claus;
Then Drunken Disorder, big with his liquid bulk
Of unzipped incompetence and vomit and sleep.
And now comes Salutary Hatred, self-beshitten;
And Anarchy that acts, with Apathy his twin
That lets be acted; and Narcosis in his kinds,
That works the doorway to the double dream
Where pose the caterpillar and the butterfly
Their contradictions to the sunshine or the shroud.

The priesthood serenely appraises the secrets
And grades them according to order and harmony,
Establishing values, deriving from every vision
Its proper doctrine: from drunkenness a jail,
From sexual license the institution of wedlock,
From anarchy and apathy the armed services,
Industrial development from drugged sleep,
And from hatred the holy mystery of the law;
Absorbing outrage into probability,
Improving virtue from the average of vice.

Now avant garde movies are made, money is given
For receiving the sages and making them at home
In the accursed culture; with subversive civility
The bride-price is paid that the City be saved.
And the dreams of the desert are digested in art.
To reactionary mirages now the sages retire
In their neo-classical Cadillacs, miraculous
Ranches arise on the sands, and roses red and white
Bloom in the dust at the door; the sages get busy
Revising their visions conformably with fact.

While in the sacred precincts now the scribes
Already expound the Word that was without the world
An idiot star, a shining in chaos underived,
That now is marketable cosmos, and a cause
To be fought for and against, to be taught in schools
With grades, degrees, and fellowships, and gowns,
And hides, and hoods, by master ham and doctor clown;
Already in the colleges the Word that was no word
Is processed from the podium by professors in prose,
And dedicated scholars in the graduate schools

Busy to squeeze the Absurd and divide the Void
Into courses given for credit, that the generations
May batten on the bitter diet of the desert
Until the secret desire of their blood shall be
To property protected by the blue police
Whose order guards the graves beneath the vaults
Beneath the banks, whose houses now are glass
Contempting stones; in whose aquarian light, subdued,
Glow golden secretaries inaccessible on stilted heels,
And savage action paintings hanging patient on the walls.

The Phi Beta Kappa poem at Harvard
15th June, 1965

A Modern Poet

Crossing at rush hour the Walt Whitman Bridge,
He stopped at the Walt Whitman Shopping Center
And bought a paperback copy of *Leaves of Grass*.
Fame *is* the spur, he figured; given a Ford
Foundation Fellowship, he'd buy a Ford.

On the Platform

Account of your what critics call Prose Style,
And all them balanced periods wherein
You imitate a thought that can't make up its mind,
People invite you, every little while,
To tell them on the one hand and the other hand
What kind of shape the world is in.

You tell 'em: Bad. And they like that.
A tape recorder takes it down, puts you on ice
For future reverence. There is applause,
And you make like you are tipping your hat
And smiling go. They've got you taped because
Later they'll want to waste the same time twice.

Takes guts, to go on record time after time
Affirming all them contradictions which
Within the self belong. Sometimes in rime,
Too. They like it, they want to make you rich,
'Cause when you stand up there before the mike
You talk the way you really think, like Ike.

Cybernetics

Now you are ready to build your human brain.
You have studied the plan, and taken inventory
Of all the pieces you found in the kit.
The first brain won't be inexpensive or
Compact; covering most of Central Park
With these tiny transistors, it will cost
A sum slightly in excess of the Gross
National Product for Nineteen Fifty-Nine;
But that is not a scientific problem,
For later brains will reproduce themselves
At less expense, on a far smaller scale,
Bringing down average costs in the long run.
Screwdriver ready? But before you start,
Consider, helmsman, what a brain requires.
A human brain has always needed blood,
And always got it, too, in plenty; but
That problem occupies a later stage;
Right now, some elementary decisions.

It must, of course, be absolutely free,
That's been determined, and accordingly
You will program it to program itself,
Set up its own projects and work them out,
Adjusting what it does tomorrow by
The feedback from today, and casually
Repairing yesterday's disasters with
The earliest possible editorials.
It must assure itself, by masterful
Administration of the unforeseen,
That everything works according to plan,
And that, as a General from the Pentagon
Recently told Congress, "The period

Of greatest danger lies ahead." This way
Alone it will be able to preserve
Anxiety and sloth in a see-saw balance,
Provoking the flow of both adrenalin
And phlegm (speaking electronically),
Whence its conflicting elements achieve
A fair symbiosis, something between
The flood of power and the drouth of fear:
A mediocrity, or golden mean,
Maybe at best the stoic *apatheia*.

At the same time, to be a human brain,
It has to have a limiting tradition,
Which may be simple and parochial
(A memory of Main Street in the sunlight)
But should be unequivocal as well:
"My country right or wrong," or "I believe
In free enterprise and high tariffs,"
Or "God will punish me if I suck my thumb."
Something like that. You will provide also
A rudimentary view of history:
One eyeless bust of Cicero or Caesar,
A Washington Crossing the Delaware,
The Driving of the Golden Railroad Spike;
Maybe a shot of Lenin tombed in glass.
It need not be much, but it must be there.

Maybe you want a more ambitious brain?
One that can keep all history in mind,
Revise the whole to fit one added fact,
And do this in three hundredths of a second
While making accurate predictions of
Price fluctuations for the next six months?

Perfectly possible, and well within
The technical means at hand. Only, there's this:
It runs you into much more money for
Circuits of paradox and contradiction.
Your vessels of antinomian wrath alone
Run into millions; and you can't stop there,
You've got to add at every junction point
Auxiliary systems that will handle doubt,
Switches of agony that are On and Off
At the same time, and limited-access
Blind alleys full of inefficient gods
And marvelous devils. No, you're asking the
Impossible, Dostoevsky described it:
"A Petersburg intellectual with a toothache."
Better to settle for the simpler model.
You could put a man on the moon for less.

O helmsman! in your hands how equal now
Weigh opportunity and obligation.
A chance to mate those monsters of the Book,
The lion and serpent hidden from our sight
Through centuries of shadowed speculation.
What if the Will's a baffled, mangy lion,
Or Thought's no adder but a strong constrictor?
It is their offspring that we care about,
That marvelous mirror where our modest wit
Shall show gigantic. Will he uproot cities,
Or sit indoors on a rainy day and mope?
Will he decide against us, or want love?
How shall we see him, or endure his stride
Into our future bellowing Nil Mirari
While all his circuits click, propounding new
Solutions to the riddle of the Sphinx?

Keeping Informed in D.C.

Each morning when I break my buttered toast
Across the columns of the *Morning Post*,
I am astounded by the ways in which
Mankind has managed once again to bitch
Things up to a degree that yesterday
Had looked impossible. Not far away
From dreams of mine, I read this dream of theirs,
And think: It's true, we *are* the bankrupt heirs
Of all the ages, history *is* the bunk.
If you do not believe in all this junk,
If you're not glad things are not as they are,
    You can wipe your arse on the *Evening Star*.

The Great Society, Mark X

The engine and transmission and the wheels
Are made of greed, fear, and invidiousness
Fueled by super-pep high octane money
And lubricated with hypocrisy,
Interior upholstery is all handsewn
Of the skins of children of the very poor,
Justice and mercy, charity and peace,
Are optional items at slight extra cost,
The steering gear is newsprint powered by
Expediency but not connected with
The wheels, and finally there are no brakes.

However, the rear-view mirror and the horn
Are covered by our lifetime guarantee.

The Dream of Flying Comes of Age

Remember those wingovers and loops and spins?
Forbidden. Heavy, powerful, and solemn,
Our scheduled transports keep the straight and level.
It's not the joystick now, but the control column.

Grace To Be Said at the Supermarket

That God of ours, the Great Geometer,
Does something for us here, where He hath put
(if you want to put it that way) things in shape,
Compressing the little lambs in orderly cubes,
Making the roast a decent cylinder,
Fairing the tin ellipsoid of a ham,
Getting the luncheon meat anonymous
In squares and oblongs with the edges beveled
Or rounded (streamlined, maybe, for greater speed).

Praise Him, He hath conferred aesthetic distance
Upon our appetites, and on the bloody
Mess of our birthright, our unseemly need,
Imposed significant form. Through Him the brutes
Enter the pure Euclidean kingdom of number,
Free of their bulging and blood-swollen lives
They come to us holy, in cellophane
Transparencies, in the mystical body,

That we may look unflinchingly on death
As the greatest good, like a philosopher should.

August, 1945

Feeble Caligula! to say
You wished mankind one only neck.
The dying guards might dance that day
At Auschwitz and at Maidanek,
Seeing their bloody seed begin to swell
Where the two cities fell.

That was our deed, without us done.
Great murder in the earth was set
That day to grow, and for us won
A present freedom to regret
Necessity, that once had made us, blind,
The saviors of mankind.

The pluming shadow of that plant,
A tragic actor now grown tall
To toppling, sounds the haughty cant
And birdlike flutes of sorrow, all
That power cracked at the root and manifest
In the burnt Phoenix' nest.

Christmas Morning

I snuggle down under the electric blanket
Turned onto high, and sneak a look at the dawn
With one pure fire of a sinking star
Over the gray snow blanketing the lawn;

Now once again the Child is born. Downstairs
The children are early out of bed, ready
To tear the wrappings from the usual junk
Where helpless love became commodity

As knowing nothing else to do. Downstreet
The lit-up crèche before the Baptist Church
Is lapped in filthy snow, its figures stained
And leaning at a hazard in the lurch

Of headstones heaved by frost; theirs is the strength
That makes the life-size plastic toy machine-
guns on which even a moment's happiness
Depends, with all the safety of the scene—

The whitened village on the greeting card
Sent by the Bank—against the alien priest
Who drenches his white robes in gasoline
And blazes merrily in the snowy East.

Part III

Figures

The Flame of a Candle

Old fabulous rendering up,
Light on a shoestring, fire out of fat
Consuming oil and cup
Together, what

Miracle! the soul's splatter and flap
Aloft, enlightened lamb
That spurting through the beastly trap
Is able to say *I am*
That I am—

Our fathers lived on these
Desperate certainties;
Ate manna in the desert, it is said,
And are dead.

Between the Window and the Screen

Between the window and the screen
A black fly climbed and fell
All day, then toward nightfall
Despaired and died.

Next morning there one tiny ant
Raced up and down the screen
Holding above his head
That huge black hulk.

I helped not, nor oversaw the end
Ordained to the black ant
Bearing the thin-winged heavy death
Aloft as a proud flag,

But write it out for you to read
And take what it may yield;
No harder emblem had
Achilles' shield.

Decorated Skull in a University Museum

Original artist, you have become
The subject of yourself, you have contained
Your own content, and in your vanity
No thought is not my own.

As when one looks at a celestial globe,
So all things here, big doll, turn inside out
With you. Instead of eyes, your spiral shells
Go spiraling standing still

In endless gaze, and your cosmetic clay
Rounds out a cosmos all disguises but
Express. *Magna cum laude*, modern poet,
You Master of Fine Arts!

Dead River

Passive and dark, dead river,
Drifting beneath the images
Received in one sole moving eye,
Beginning nowhere, never
Arriving, ever to be done;
Reflecting back in black
The leaves, the sky, the silver sun,
Dead river, you still give
Your still moving negative
Down to the still glade
Where the beaver has made
His sill of speckled mud
And saplings silver-dry,
Deliverance of the sun,
Dead river, past which never,
Dead river, beyond which not,

While summer dries away in gold
Jeweled with bright and buzzing flies.

The Rope's End

Unraveling a rope
You begin at an end.
Taking the finished work
You pick it to its bits,

Straightening out the crossed,
Deriving many from one,
Moving forward in time
And backward in idea,

Reaching to finer elements
And always thinner filaments,
From rope to cord to thread
And so on down to splinters

No longer serpentine
That break instead of coil
And that will blow away
Before a little breath,

Having attained the first
Condition, being dust,
No longer resembling rope
Or cord or thread or hair,

And following no line:
Incapable of knot or wave
Or tying things together
Or making anything secure,

Unable to bind, or whip,
Or hang till dead. All this
In the last analysis
Is crazy man's work,

Admitted, who can leave
Nothing continuous
Since Adam's fall
Unraveled all.

Projection

They were so amply beautiful, the maps,
With their blue rivers winding to the sea,
So calmly beautiful, who could have blamed
Us for believing, bowed to our drawing boards,
In one large and ultimate equivalence,
One map that challenged and replaced the world?

Our punishment? To stand here, on these ladders,
Dizzy with fear, not daring to look down,
Glue on our fingers, in our hair and eyes,
Piecing together the crackling, sticky sheets
We hope may paper yet the walls of space
With pictures any child can understand.

In the Black Museum

When all analogies are broken
The scene grows strange again. At last
There is only one of everything.

This I had seen a long time coming
In my landscape of blunt instruments,
My garden of bearded herms.

For years I had carried a traveler's word
That he had seen in Fiji "sacred stones
That had children, but the children were stones,"

And did not know till now what silent thing
That hard, two-headed saying said: one mask
To every skull, that is the end of art.

These uncertainty relations now refine
Themselves toward ever-greater accuracy,
Unreadable in any antinomian sense,

Conceding nothing to a metaphysics;
As in my dream one night a sliding door
Opened upon another sliding door;

Or as two mirrors vacuum-locked together
Exclude, along with all the world,
A light to see it by. Reflect on that.

The Race

So many tortoises
Unwind and wind
The clue of the wheel
On the road of the race

In each cool shadow
Under the shoulder
Of cedar and spruce
In each cool shadow
Of granite ledge
By green still pool
Under the shoulder
The failed favorite
Sprinter's asleep

He dreams of being
Wherever he is

While swish and swish
The silent families
Mounted in glass
Facing the front
Are strictly passing
Away on the slab
Of their fated freeway
Offering cokes
With cigarettes

Their eyeballs rolling
Along that road
Of the dead cats
And frightened flies

Mirages perpetual
Of asphalt pools

Sightseers

Where history was
Hordes of them come
With the black boxes
Strapped to the neck,
Borne on the breast,
Tabernacle or pyx
Priestly with symbols
In silver and black,
With numbers incised
And cryptic sayings
About the light.
These portable shrines
Covered in skins
They aim at all
Remarkable things:
Click, the Vatican,
Click, the Sphinx,
Click, in the Badlands,
The enormous nostrils
Of the Fathers
                    Click
Sometimes they dream
Of looking alive,
Of being released
To the ripple and flash
Of a fiery world
Where the dragonfly
Glitters and goes
And the gold sun sinks
In the oil black film
Of a pool, forever

Evanescent, but
No: reflexion
Has intervened, and
The dark will won
Again, in the box
That knows no now,
In the mind bowed down
Among the shadows
Of shadowy things,
Itself a shadow
Less sure than they.

Thought

Thought is seldom itself
And never itself alone.
It is the mind turning
To images. Maybe
Idea is like the day,
Being both everywhere
And always in one place.

Leaves shaken in the wind
Rattle the light till shadows
Elide, and yet the grass
Bends to the weight of the wind
And not the shadows' weight.
The minnow-waves can mingle
In shallows at the shore
As if they were no matter,
Until they peak and break,
Taking the sunlight up
In a shatter of spray.

And mind in some such way
Passing across the world
May make its differences
At last unselfishly
The casualties of cause:
  It's likeness changes.

Style

Flaubert wanted to write a novel
About nothing. It was to have no subject
And be sustained upon style alone,
Like the Holy Ghost cruising above
The abyss, or like the little animals
In Disney cartoons who stand upon a branch
That breaks, but do not fall
Till they look down. He never wrote that novel,
And neither did he write another one
That would have been called *La Spirale*,
Wherein the hero's fortunes were to rise
In dreams, while his waking life disintegrated.

Even so, for these two books
We thank the master. They can be read,
With difficulty, in the spirit alone,
Are not so wholly lost as certain works
Burned at Alexandria, flooded at Florence,
And are never taught at universities.
Moreover, they are not deformed by style,
That fire that eats what it illuminates.

Celestial Globe

This is the world
Without the world.
I hold it in my hand,
A hollow sphere
Of childlike blue
With magnitudes of stars.
There in its utter dark
The singing planets go,
And the sun, great source,
Is blazing forth his fires
Over the many-oceaned
And river-shining earth
Whereon I stand
Balancing this ball
Upon my hand.

It is the universe,
The Turning One.
As if children at the Museum
Should watch some amateur
Copying Rembrandt's painting
Of Aristotle contemplating
The skull of Homer, that
Dark fire fountaining forth
The twin poems of the war
And of the journey home—
As if the children stood
In the mind of Homer
As on the ball of the world
Where every inside's out.

It is the world
Beyond the world.
Holding it in my hand,
I wear it on my head
As a candle wears a pumpkin
At Halloween, when children
Rise as the dead; only
It has no human features,
No access to its depths
Whatever, where it keeps
In the utter dark
The candle of the sun,
The candle of the mind,
Twin fires that together
Turn all things inside out.

One Way

The way a word does when
It senses on one side
A thing and on the other
A thought; at either side
It glances and goes deep
Together; like sunlight
On marble, on burnished wood,
That seems to be coming from
Within the surface and
To be one substance with it—
That is one way of doing
One's being in a world
Whose being is both thought
And thing, where neither thing
Nor thought will do alone
Till either answers other;
Two lovers in the night
Each sighing other's name
Whose alien syllables
Become synonymous
For all their mortal night
And their embodied day:
    Fire in the diamond,
    Diamond in the dark.

Part IV

The Blue Swallows

The Blue Swallows

Across the millstream below the bridge
Seven blue swallows divide the air
In shapes invisible and evanescent,
Kaleidoscopic beyond the mind's
Or memory's power to keep them there.

"History is where tensions were,"
"Form is the diagram of forces."
Thus, helplessly, there on the bridge,
While gazing down upon those birds—
How strange, to be above the birds!—
Thus helplessly the mind in its brain
Weaves up relation's spindrift web,
Seeing the swallows' tails as nibs
Dipped in invisible ink, writing . . .

Poor mind, what would you have them write?
Some cabalistic history
Whose authorship you might ascribe
To God? to Nature? Ah, poor ghost,
You've capitalized your Self enough.
That villainous William of Occam
Cut out the feet from under that dream
Some seven centuries ago.
It's taken that long for the mind
To waken, yawn and stretch, to see
With opened eyes emptied of speech
The real world where the spelling mind
Imposes with its grammar book
Unreal relations on the blue
Swallows. Perhaps when you will have
Fully awakened, I shall show you

A new thing: even the water
Flowing away beneath those birds
Will fail to reflect their flying forms,
And the eyes that see become as stones
Whence never tears shall fall again.

O swallows, swallows, poems are not
The point. Finding again the world,
That is the point, where loveliness
Adorns intelligible things
Because the mind's eye lit the sun.

The May Day Dancing

The kindergarten children first come forth
In couples dressed as little brides and grooms.
By dancing in, by dancing round and out,
They braid the Maypole with a double thread;
Keep time, keep faith, is what the music says.

The corporal piano now leads out
Successively the older boys and girls,
Grade after grade, all for the dancing paired,
All dressed in the fashion of forgotten folk;
Those nymphs and shepherds, maybe, never were.

And all the parents standing in a ring,
With cameras some, and some with only eyes,
Attend to the dancing's measurable rule
Bemused, or hypnotized, so that they see
Not seven classes of children, but only one,

One class of children seven times again
That ever enters on the dancing floor
One year advanced in their compliant skill
To patterns ever with more varied styles
Clothing the naked order of the bass.

Some here relate the May with wanton rites,
Some with the Haymarket Riots, some with nothing
Beyond the present scene and circumstance
Which by the camera's thin incisive blade
They hope to take a frozen section through,

Keeping their child with one foot on the ground
And one foot off, and with a solemn face
Or one bewildered between grin and tears,
As many times repeating time and faith
He follows the compulsions of the dance

Around the brilliant morning with the sun,
The dance that leads him out to bring him home,
The May Day dance that tramples down the grass
And raises dust, that braids a double thread
Around the pole, in the great room of the sun.

The Breaking of Rainbows

Oil is spilling down the little stream
Below the bridge. Heavy and slow as blood,
Or with an idiot's driveling contempt:
The spectral film unfolding, spreading forth
Prismatically in a breaking of rainbows,
Reflective radiance, marble evanescence,
It shadows the secret moves the water makes,
Creeping upstream again, then prowling down,
Sometimes asleep in the dull corners, combed
As the deep grass is combed in the stream's abandon,
And sometimes tearing open silently
Its seamless fabric in momentary shapes
Unlikened and nameless as the shapes of sky
That open with the drift of cloud, and close,
High in the lonely mountains, silently.
The curve and glitter of it as it goes
The maze of its pursuit, reflect the water
In agony under the alien, brilliant skin
It struggles to throw off and finally does
Throw off, on its frivolous purgatorial fall
Down to the sea and away, dancing and singing
Perpetual intercession for this filth—
Leaping and dancing and singing, forgiving everything.

The Beekeeper Speaks . . .

I

Bees aren't humble, they don't notably bumble,
They tend to run a touch Stakhanovite,
If you'll allow the lofty title to
A hedonist who works himself to death
Flying at every blossom in the orchard
In a madness of efficiency at pleasure,
Like a totalitarian Don Juan
In serious pursuit. The best of them
Will last out maybe six weeks of the season,
Doing the apple's business for his drink,
Until, exhausted, or with a broken wing,
He falls; and when he falls his fellow workers
Team up in tandem to bear him from the hive
And drop him in a field to starve to death:
There's that much nonsense to a hive of bees.

II

The damn fool growers used to spray their trees
So early, they drove out if not knocked off
Their native hives—a typical maneuver
For people driven by the economy
Until they finish by protecting what
They haven't got so hard they cannot have it.
So now they have to hire hives from me,
At least around this county, anyhow,
That's how it is, five bucks a hive the season,
Some fifteen hundred hives; it brings in dough
All right, and it's a way to make a living
Still has a shade of mystery about it;
People who need you come round all respectful,
But not quite friendly, maybe a little scared:
They damn well should be, it's a mystery.

III

There's not much competition in the bee
Business, because the plain sense of it is
You can't discourage bees from stinging when
They need to, which I guess is God knows when.
I got in this game young and plenty scared,
We used to wear, back then, netting and gloves,
And get stung anyhow, right through all that.
By now I never mind, I wear my sleeves
Rolled up, no net, no nothing except bees
That when you open up the skep come out
Like steam out of a boiling kettle, but
Much louder. And they carpet you all over,
It's in the cards that some of them will sting:
Maybe a couple of dozen stings a day,
By now I hardly notice any more.

IV

Anaphylactic shock, they talk about,
The doctors. They've their language, I have mine.
I might have bothered over all that once,
Until I figured if you really were
Allergic, first you'd know about it was
When you were dead. And since you weren't dead,
You'd learned the human blood is subtle stuff,
Its nature is the nature of the world
Outside the human, too, it gets a knowledge,
Borne on the poisoned point, how to become
Indifferent at first, and later on
Pleased with so powerful a nourishment
As comes from nature's winged sex and source:
The bloodstream is a venom in itself,
Sometimes I think to hear it hum in me.

V

And sometimes, too, not only in the night,
Lying awake, hearing life hum away,
But at the first of summer in the field
Releasing life and death in black and gold
Bullets that shake the petals back and forth,
And not the petals only, but the boughs,
With many-winged furies bearing futures,
I have felt myself become at first a bee,
And then the single-minded hive itself,
And after that the blossoming apple tree
Inside the violation of the swarm—
Until I am the brute and fruitful earth,
Furred with the fury of the golden horde,
And hear from far upon the field of time
The wild relentless singing of the stars.

The Mud Turtle

Out of the earth beneath the water,
Dragging over the stubble field
Up to the hilltop in the sun
On his way from water to water,
He rests an hour in the garden,
His alien presence observed by all:
His lordly darkness decked in filth
Bearded with weed like a lady's favor,
He is a black planet, another world
Never till now appearing, even now
Not quite believably old and big,
Set in the summer morning's midst
A gloomy gemstone to the sun opposed.
Our measures of him do not matter,
He would be huge at any size;
And neither does the number of his years,
The time he comes from doesn't count.

When the boys tease him with sticks
He breaks the sticks, striking with
As great a suddenness as speed;
Fingers and toes would snap as soon,
Says one of us, and the others shudder.
Then when they turn him on his back
To see the belly heroically yellow,
He throws himself fiercely to his feet,
Brings down the whole weight of his shell,
Spreads out his claws and digs himself in
Immovably, invulnerably,
But for the front foot on the left,
Red-budded, with the toes torn off.
So over he goes again, and shows

Us where a swollen leech is fastened
Softly between plastron and shell.
Nobody wants to go close enough
To burn it loose; he can't be helped
Either, there is no help for him
As he makes it to his feet again
And drags away to the meadow's edge.
We see the tall grass open and wave
Around him, it closes, he is gone
Over the hill toward another water,
Bearing his hard and chambered hurt
Down, down, down, beneath the water,
Beneath the earth beneath. He takes
A secret wound out of the world.

Summer's Elegy

Day after day, day after still day,
The summer has begun to pass away.
Starlings at twilight fly clustered and call,
And branches bend, and leaves begin to fall.
The meadow and the orchard grass are mown,
And the meadowlark's house is cut down.

The little lantern bugs have doused their fires,
The swallows sit in rows along the wires.
Berry and grape appear among the flowers
Tangled against the wall in secret bowers,
And cricket now begins to hum the hours
Remaining to the passion's slow procession
Down from the high place and the golden session
Wherein the sun was sacrificed for us.
A failing light, no longer numinous,
Now frames the long and solemn afternoons
Where butterflies regret their closed cocoons.
We reach the place unripe, and made to know
As with a sudden knowledge that we go
Away forever, all hope of return
Cut off, hearing the crackle of the burn-
ing blade behind us, and the terminal sound
Of apples dropping on the dry ground.

Two Girls

I saw again in a dream the other night
Something I saw in daylight years ago,
A path in the rainy woods, a shaft of light,
And two girls walking together through shadow,
Through dazzle, till I lost them on their way
In gloom embowering beyond the glade.
The bright oblivion that belongs to day
Covered their steps, nothing of them remained,

Until the darkness brought them forth again
To the rainy glitter and the silver light,
The ancient leaves that had not fallen then.
Two girls, going forever out of sight,
Talking of lovers, maybe, and of love:
Not that blind life they'd be the mothers of.

For Robert Frost, in the Autumn, in Vermont

All on the mountains, as on tapestries
Reversed, their threads unreadable though clear,
The leaves turn in the volume of the year.
Your land becomes more brilliant as it dies.

The puzzled pilgrims come, car after car,
With cameras loaded for epiphanies;
For views of failure to take home and prize,
The dying tourists ride through realms of fire.

"To die is gain," a virgin's tombstone said;
That was New England, too, another age
That put a higher price on maidenhead
If brought in dead; now on your turning page
The lines blaze with a constant light, displayed
As in the maple's cold and fiery shade.

The Sweeper of Ways

All day, a small mild Negro man with a broom
Sweeps up the leaves that fall along the paths.
He carries his head to one side, looking down
At his leaves, at his broom like a windy beard
Curled with the sweeping habit. Over him
High haughty trees, the hickory and ash,
Dispense their more leaves easily, or else
The district wind, hunting hypocrisy,
Tears at the summer's wall and throws down leaves
To witness of a truth naked and cold.

Hopeless it looks, on these harsh, hastening days
Before the end, to finish all those leaves
Against time. But the broom goes back and forth
With a tree's patience, as though naturally
Erasers would speak the language of pencils.
A thousand thoughts fall on the same blank page,
Though the wind blows them back, they go where he
Directs them, to the archives where disorder
Blazes and a pale smoke becomes the sky.
The ways I walk are splendidly free of leaves.

We meet, we smile good morning, say the weather
Whatever. On a rainy day there'll be
A few leaves stuck like emblems on the walk;
These too he brooms at till they come unstuck.
Masters, we carry our white faces by
In silent prayer, Don't hate me, on a wave-
length which his broom's antennae perfectly
Pick up, we know ourselves so many thoughts
Considered by a careful, kindly mind
Which can do nothing, and is doing that.

Small Moment

Isaiah 54:7

Death is serious,
or else all things are serious
except death. A player who dies
automatically disqualifies
for the finals. If there were no death
nothing could be taken seriously,
not truth, not beauty, but that is not
a situation which we need to face.
Men invented the gods, but they
discovered death; therefore, although
the skull is said to grin, the flesh
is serious, and frowns, for the world
is not a stage. And the gay spirit, gone
through wisdom to absurdity,
welcomes the light that shudders in the leaves
in all weathers and at any season,
since love, the pure, unique, and useless virtue,
climbs in the stalk and concentrates this dust
until it takes the light and shines
with the fat blood of death. So men say
that flowers light the sun, and so also,
when Theseus fought Antiope,
the battlefield became the marriage bed.
When you have known how this may be
you have already lived forever,
forsaken once in the small moment,
but gathered with great mercies after.

Firelight in Sunlight

Firelight in sunlight, silver-pale
Streaming with emerald, copper, sapphire
Ribbons and rivers, banners, fountains;
They rise, they run swiftly away.

Now apple logs unlock their sunlight
In the many-windowed room to meet
New sunlight falling in silvered gold
Through the fern-ice forest of the glass
Whose tropic surface light may pierce
If not the eye. O early world,
Still Daphne of the stubborn wood
Singing Apollo's song in light,
O pulsing constancies of flame
Warping a form along the log's
Slowly disintegrating face
Crackled and etched, so quickly aged,
These are my mysteries to see
And say and celebrate with words
In orders until now reserved.

For light is in the language now,
Carbon and sullen diamond break
Out of the glossary of earth
In holy signs and scintillations,
Release their fiery emblems to
Renewal's room and morning's room
Where sun and fire once again
Phase in the figure of the dance
From far beginnings here returned,
Leapt from the maze at the forest's heart,
O moment where the lost is found!

Interiors

Small flame pointing, shadowing, picking out
Black lacquer, bronze, blue velvet, a tassel
That sweeps the chequered floor. God of battles,
Bless these Thy banners. Smoke and the smell of fat
Ascending to cold turbulence over us,
A cold wind crawling the stone thresholds,
And through the cry of captains in the street
The hooded women carry uprooted canes
Into the courtyard for the fire of
Their ceremony called Burning of Wands.

The icy road, a rider drawn up at the door,
Knock echoing, what he has in hand
Peremptory, urgently magnificent,
Orders, tidings, there is never time.

So warm, so clear at the line of corded velvet
The marvelous flesh, its faster rise and fall,
Sigh in the throat, the mouth fallen open,
The knees fallen open, the heavy flag of the skirt
Urgently gathered together, quick, so quick,
Black lacquer, bronze, blue velvet, gleam
Of pewter in a tarnishing light, the book
Of the body lying open at the last leaf,
Where the spirit and the bride say, Come,
As from deep mirrors on the hinted wall
Beyond these shadows, a small flame sprouts.

DATE DUE

PRINTED IN U.S.A.